AF316726

David and the Cookies Dilemma

By Debra R. Shreve

This story is about a young boy named David who kept a lot of secrets from his mother Joanne.

One day, his mother was in the kitchen baking cookies. They smelled so good. David wanted to eat one so bad, but his mother said to him: "No cookies until after dinner."
MiLK
sugar

David was sitting at the kitchen table all by himself with those cookies on a plate in front of him.

David was thinking to himself: "Those cookies would taste really good with a nice cold cup of milk."

His mother was in
the basement washing
clothes.

What do you think is going to happen next? Turn to the next page and see!

Since there was no one around, David decided to eat three of the cookies and tell his mother that they fell on the floor and he threw them in the garbage.

Do you think this was a good thing to do because no one was around to see him do it?

What would you
have done if you were
David?

Sometimes our wants can get the best of us. It can feel so right and look so good. . .
. . .but it might not be the right thing to do at that time, or any time. . .

When someone thinks
about doing something
long enough, whether
good or bad, they are
going to do it because
they made up their mind

Do you think David
made up his mind
to eat the cookies
and lie to his mother?

David thought he got away with telling his mother a lie, but his conscience got the best of him.

He begins to think to himself that he should have eaten all the cookies. David questions himself on how just three cookies could fall on the floor while the others stayed on the plate. His story begins to fall apart and not make any sense.

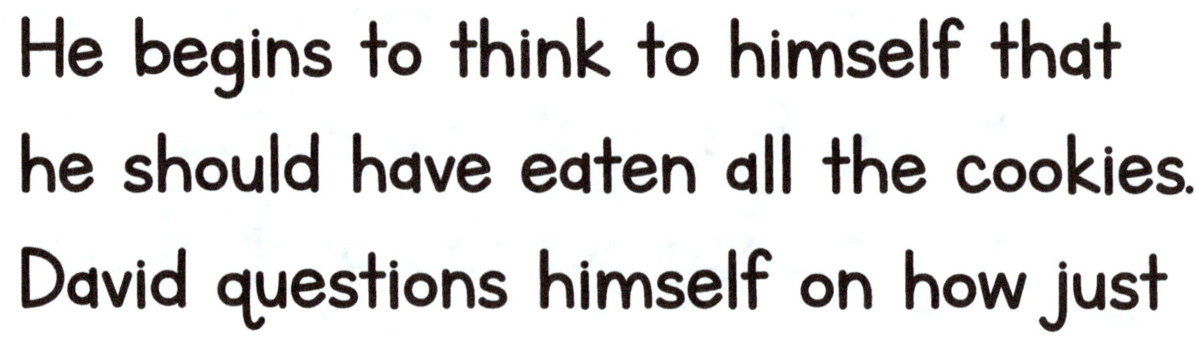

David's story seems to get worse the more he thought about it. Fibbing makes bad smells. His lies begin to stink.

David realizes that just because things seem to look good doesn't mean it's always the right thing to do.

David became so worried about everything he had done, including making up a lie to tell his mother. David's stomach began to hurt.

At this point, David decided to tell his mother the truth and say he was sorry for everything he did.

David's mother was very proud
that he told the truth.

Finally, David was moving in the right direction. David's sadness turned into joy because he made the wrong thing right! No more stomach ache!

Things to ponder on:

If David had done what his mother said in the first place, he would have enjoyed the chocolate chip cookies after dinner without the drama!